HOW TO
SUCK
AT BUSINESS
WITHOUT REALLY TRYING

This book is not meant to be taken seriously and is not for those who would prefer to take the views and opinions of the fictional protagonist as gospel.

Unfortunately, this book is inspired by true events.

www.mascotbooks.com

HOW TO **SUCK** AT BUSINESS WITHOUT REALLY TRYING

For more information, please contact:
Mascot Books
620 Herndon Parkway, Suite 320
Herndon, VA 20170
info@mascotbooks.com

Library of Congress Control Number: 2021907799

CPSIA Code: PRFRE0621A
ISBN-13: 978-1-64543-709-3

Printed in Canada

Dedicated to:

Myself, without whom none of this would be possible.

HOW TO
SUCK
AT BUSINESS
WITHOUT REALLY TRYING

MARAH ARCHER,
DOWNTRODDEN BY THE WORLD'S "BEST" BOSS

CONTENTS

Foreward   1

Introduction   3
Chapter 1: Overview Of A Business   7
Chapter 2: Company Culture   13
Chapter 3: Communication   19
Chapter 4: Human Resources (HR)   25
Chapter 5: Name Drop To Show Who's Boss   45
Chapter 6: Strategy   47
Chapter 7: Marketing & Business Development   59
Chapter 8: Project Management   67
Chapter 9: Tech & Big Data   79
Chapter 10: Leadership   89
Chapter 11: Starting A Start-Up   99
Chapter 12: Closing Comments   103

Acknowledgement   107
Glossary of Terms   111

FOREWARD

I WROTE THIS BOOK so that people would stop asking me questions. My experience wasn't free for me, and it shouldn't be free for anyone else. I don't consider myself a scholar, but I'm too smart not to be one. I'm on the boards of several start-ups, and I teach business classes at a high-profile university. Hint: *the* university might use the word *the* in its title.

I wrote this book as an answer to all the questions I receive about starting and running a business. I require my students to buy my book for all of my classes, and when a start-up founder emails me with questions, I reply with a link to purchase this book. What you have in your hands is gold. But realize that gold has weight to it. I tackle the hard stuff about business that everyone else is unwilling to say, and I prove my points with real experience.

My editors made me add footnotes and side notes to the layout of this book. They said if I didn't put footnotes in that I would be "plagiarizing." Most of the people I refer to are people I disagree with. I wouldn't want to plagiarize them even if I could. Side notes include important information that's not directly related to what I'm talking about. My editor told me those were "tangents," but I told my editor that there would be absolutely no math in my book. Math is for suckers who lick lollipops instead of pussy. There are also HUGE QUOTES in this book. These are nuggets of wisdom that I told my editor I wanted big and bold.

INTRODUCTION

Life is full of hardships, pimp slaps, and sorrow.
—Coolio

I'VE BEEN TOLD that I don't know what I'm doing. Horseshit. There's no way in Satan's marbly asshole that I've accomplished the things that I've accomplished without knowing what I'm doing. Like the font of this book. I was told what I wanted was too difficult to read and had to settle for this instead. Trust me, in life, you'll have to be bold.

In business, I've constantly had to make **BOLD** choices. And it's not been easy. I've had to pull a woman out of a molester's arms. I've had to hire people and tell them that they're doing an okay job. But it's not impossible, and I'm sure someone else like me could do it, too. That's who this book is for. To the mini me out there, shine on.

I had a tough childhood. I was shy. My mom made me do all of my homework, and my dad always forced me to watch *Fantasy Island*. None of the girls noticed me in middle school or high school. I bet they wish they had now. I was just your typical boy next door. Growing up in a small midwestern town, I knew there was more to life than my sweet suburb, and I was inspired by the pain I felt when I listened to rap music.

WHEN GIVEN A GIFT, TAKE IT AND RUN. NO TAKESIES BACKSIES

Rap music is my mantra. I quote bits to myself to keep my head in the game. But enough about me. Let's talk about my work. I played NCAA Division 1 football for Michigan. I learned that life is a football game and that everything, EVERY lesson in life, can be taught from a football field. That includes business. I graduated with a BS in interdisciplinary studies. I couldn't tell you what I learned, but it didn't matter. After graduation, I immediately got a job at a consulting firm. I worked with top businesses that create all the brands you can buy in a superstore. I shocked the firm with my capabilities and charm—so they paid my way through grad school. I got an MBA and quit the firm on my graduation day. **When given a gift, take it and run. No takesies backsies.**

When I run, I run fast. And boy, did I. I ran all the way to LA. That's Los Angeles, not Louisiana, for all the less-fortunate kiddos. So, I ran so far away, and I landed a job for a VC. (Again, for the poor, dumb kids, that's venture capital.) I nailed that gig. I was soon promoted to managing partner. But, I fell out of love with the powers that be. We just didn't see eye to eye on the direction of the company. I moved back to the Midwest and started my own company with my millions. And I'm crushing it.

That's it. That's this book. A how-to business guide. I have lots of advice based on my real business experience. But hey, this is just my experience . . . it's not like I'm successful or anything.

CHAPTER 1

OVERVIEW OF A BUSINESS

Real Gs move in silence, like lasagna.
—Lil Wayne

CHOOSING AN INDUSTRY

I STARTED A BUSINESS in an industry that I don't give a shit about (animation). When starting a business, choosing an industry is the least important decision. Take me, for example. I can start a business in any industry—no passion or experience required. Here's how: I hired people to figure it out for me.

> Side Note: My employees aren't even experts in animation. I hired a few people, put the fear of God in them, and watched them create the company for me. Now, not all of their ideas are great; some of them suck. But mostly, I get something I can work with. Most importantly, I always take the credit for their work. The greatest compliment I can give one of my employees is passing one of their ideas off as my own. It shows that I truly value the idea. And their ideas are my property.

Every thought my employees think, I own, because any work done in my office is "work-for-hire." And that's my favorite section of the Employee Handbook.

CHOOSING A LEGAL STRUCTURE

Do what's best for your bank account. Personally, my business is "failing" and will always lose money. Because I'm the sole investor, it's in my best interest for the company to perpetually lose money so that I get a tax write-off. My biggest concern is my K-1s. As long as I file my taxes and get a massive tax write-off, I'm in good shape. Also, did I mention that I loan my company money? Not only do I get a decent tax break from owning a company with zero profit, but I also make money off the company by loaning it money and getting paid interest. This is all perfectly legal. Thank you, Uncle Sam.

CHOOSING PEOPLE

I hire people that aspire to be like me. Of course, those people are not as smart as I am or as wealthy as I am, but they can try. And they should. I also hire people that are not nearly as clever as I am. My creative director, Dan, can't even chew gum. The man's a moron. In the hiring process, I keep posting jobs even if I'm not actively hiring. It keeps the community wanting to know what's happening. And if my assistant reaches out to schedule an interview, the applicant is thrilled that he finally has a meeting with me after a year.

I'm the only person that interviews and hires new employees. It's imperative that applicants meet the leadership of the company. My employees have suggested that others should interview applicants. For example, my business manager, Sabrina, suggested that Dan interview all 3D modeling applicants to determine skill level and "fit." It's my company, and I can damn well determine who fits and who doesn't. Besides, that's not how I run things on an organizational level. I hire more people for a given role than I need and let them duke it out. It's the modern business version of Darwin's survival of the fittest.

MAKE PLANS TO MAKE PLANS TO MAKE PLANS

CHOOSING SCOPE / PURPOSE / MISSION / VISION / DIRECTION / BUSINESS FOCUS

Having a clearly defined scope, purpose, mission, vision, direction, or business focus is a surefire way to ruin a company. The purpose of my business is to dick around. At my animation studio, we offer services that seem to be an inch deep and a mile wide. We're like the restaurant you see along an interstate with a big sign that reads "Restaurant: Fish, Steak, Spaghetti, Sushi." Everyone stops to eat there because it's the only food place along the highway, and it caters to every person's cravings in the car. Sabrina is always approaching me and suggesting that I choose one thing that we do because she says that by doing so much, the company has no strengths. I say, "Sabrina, **we are the restaurant on the interstate, and our art is the stinky fish on the menu.**" My point is that it's important not to alienate any prospective client. That's why my studio does it all—I can't go into too much detail, because I don't understand it myself, but we do it all.

ORGANIZATIONAL CHANGE MANAGEMENT (OCM)

I recently came upon this term while talking to some PhD business know-it-all. OCM is nonsense. Organizational change should happen when I say so. I fly in and out of the office about once a week. When I come, my employees had better be ready for all hell to break loose. It's always necessary to whip those kids into shape. And I don't need a process or documentation for the reasons why and how I run my business. It's just not good practice. Nothing would get done.

One thing I do respect is making plans. I don't call it

"analysis paralysis;" I call it "analysis of analysis." I keep Sabrina and my tech guy Rick busy by asking them to build budgets and make plans. Otherwise, they wouldn't have anything to do. I ask them to make plans. Then we meet, and I give them a note. Then they make another budget. Then we meet, and I give them two more notes. Then they make another budget. And the cycle continues. I ask them to **make plans to make plans to make plans.** It's crucial that we spin our wheels. I've heard other, less successful business gurus suggest failing and failing quickly. That's the same as telling someone to give up immediately. I don't want to fail to learn.

WE ARE THE RESTAURANT ON THE INTERSTATE AND OUR ART IS THE STINKY FISH ON THE MENU

IF EVERYTHING IS GOING WELL IN YOUR BUSINESS, THERE'S SOMETHING WRONG

CHAPTER 2

COMPANY CULTURE

Everything I cook tastes better than yo' momma's nipples.
—*Coolio*

I DESPISE THE TERM "COMPANY CULTURE." I'm not operating a science lab. My company isn't a petri dish, and my employees aren't lab rats. They're ants. What some call "culture" I call "spirit." Take it back to my football days: I'm the skinny little blonde in tight Spanx whose every jiggle makes the spirit tingle from head to tip. I have several tips for showing company spirit in the workplace.

SPIRIT TIP #1: SPY ON EMPLOYEES

I've recently implemented a camera system so I can see how much spirit all of my employees have. These cameras also record sound. The employees don't know that, so I get a kick out of what they have to say. For example, I told Rick that I needed a technical document created for a bid I put together for a government contract. (Not just any government contract, mind you. One that scrubs audio for the Alcohol Firearms Tobacco jokers that spy on the cartel.)

Rick created the technical document for me, but it was subpar. So, I sent him one that his predecessor (who I fired) had created and told him to make it EXACTLY like that one. He did, and that was great, but he put it on blank paper. I said to Rick, "You gotta put it on the company masthead."

For the next two days, he kept asking all the employees what a masthead is. It was hilarious. How does Rick, with a master's in computer science, not know what a masthead is? Check out the conversation I heard between Rick and Sabrina.

Rick: "He asked me to put it on the company masthead. Do you know what that is?"

Sabrina: "Masthead . . . doesn't that have something to do with a ship?"

Rick: "Does it?"

Sabrina: "I'll Google it. Yeah, it's the top of a mast of a ship."

Rick: "Then what do you think he wants?"

Sabrina: "Is he talking about letterhead?"

Rick: "Maybe?"

Sabrina: "Should we ask him?"

Rick: "No, I don't think so. I'll just put it on the company letterhead and see what he says."

I said nothing. Not even a "thanks" when he emailed it on the masthead. Which leads me to . . .

SPIRIT TIP #2: THE BUSINESS IS GREATER THAN THE SUM OF ITS EMPLOYEES

I heard Rick and Sabrina on the phone with our sound contractor, Starling, talking about the government contract.

Starling (on speaker): "I've done contracts like this before. My worry is that I'm going to be called into court as a witness to testify if the sound files were edited. I don't want to spend months in court again. I had to say no to jobs."

Sabrina: "We can certainly ask, Starling."

Rick: "I'm also concerned. Like, are we at risk if someone finds out that we're scrubbing audio? Are the drug dealers going to hunt us down and shoot us?"

Silence.

Sabrina: "I hadn't thought of that."

Starling: "I don't know."

I do take safety seriously. I just had Rick install an alarm system. We don't arm it, but it's there in case we need it. But if I have to choose between employee safety and a job, I have to get the job. How else am I going to pay my employees?

SPIRIT TIP #3: FORCE COMPANY VALUES

Create a list of company values and attributes for employees to live by. These company values aren't anything to promote. The employees should be the values and attributes that the company tells them to be. I just sit and watch.

SPIRIT TIP #4: BE WORLD CLASS

Juan is my favorite employee because he's my best artist.
What makes him the best? I have no idea. I do not pretend
to know what makes good art. Hell if I care. Juan has an
attitude problem though. He's from Guatemala—or is it Ven-
ezuela? One of those types of countries. I don't remember. A
few months ago, I gave Juan my typical pep talk: "Do better."
He seemed confused. I was prepping to go to a conference
(I wasn't really going, but pretending I was). And I told him
that I wanted to "blow the doors off the conference" with the
quality of world-class art that he needed to be doing. He still
didn't get it. Probably the language barrier.

SPIRIT TIP #5: KEEP EMPLOYEES ON THEIR TOES

It is often necessary to throw wrenches. This adds an element
of surprise to daily tasks, which is a great tool to keep employees engaged. If an employee is always guessing, then that
employee is always thinking. When in a position of power, it
may seem difficult to spot a possible wrench. Especially when
things are going well. Don't be fooled. Smooth systems and
processes are a great cover for complacency. **If everything
is going well in your business, there's something wrong**;
there's something you're not seeing. I'll give you some recent
examples that I've used at my business.

1. I asked Rick to build a website for my company. I didn't
    give him too much direction. He kept sending me
    weekly updates of his progress. So annoying. He even did
    things I told him not to do. I can't stand overachievers.

It's important to knock them off their high horses. So, I approved the first version of the website, and he moved on to a different project. Then, I told him to scrap the website and start over. It was a difficult decision because it was a great website, and it put him behind schedule on the other project. But sometimes I gotta throw wrenches.

2. I lie to my project manager, Meghan. After meetings, she sends emails to confirm follow-up actions and the deliverables I request. It causes me to be something I don't feel comfortable with being: accountable and consistent. So, after she delivers the project, I always email her to tell her she forgot something. She never does, but someday she will. It's good practice.

3. I fired an employee because the office was too quiet. I don't remember her name, but I hope she's doing well.

If all other wrenches seem to fail at engaging employees, then the best wrench to throw is nepotism. Nepotism enrages employees, and rage is an excellent tool to keep my employees talking about me. Recently, I hired my wife as a consultant at $200 an hour. Then, I paid my son nine grand within one and a half months to write a short film. When hiring a family member, the key is to overpay them. This causes my employees to incessantly gab at the office and try to suck up to me to get a raise. My plan is for the artists to start the short and then throw them onto another project just before they finish.

A few months ago, I went into the studio over the weekend and took an office chair, just to see if anyone would notice. That Monday, Rick emailed me and copied the entire staff saying that an office chair was missing. I scheduled an all-staff meeting and plodded into the office. I sat everyone down and told them that stealing would not be tolerated under any circumstances. I emailed Rick later and told him that I took the chair for business purposes.

I always keep my business at an arm's length from generating profit. Once a year, my business's bank accounts usually drop to a level that's just enough to meet the next two payrolls. Essentially, I keep enough cash on hand to keep us open for a month until I decide to swing in with another interest-bearing loan. This happened again about a month ago, and Sabrina was stressed about the amount of cash in the bank. Although I usually plan to loan my company money, I didn't tell her that. Instead, I told her to try to figure it out because she may lose her job at the end of the month. She's a good girl, but she worries too much. It's not that big of a deal if I decide to shut the place down one day. It's not like artists can't find jobs in this economy.

MY COMPANY ISN'T A PETRI DISH

CHAPTER 3

COMMUNICATION

Never let them know your next move.
—Biggie Smalls

UNFORTUNATELY, COMMUNICATION IS NECESSARY when owning a business. So, I communicate on my own terms. I see it as a game. Which game? Telephone.

Client projects and internal projects require me to be the point of contact. Again, and I can't stress this enough, my business is my business. Typical communications for client or internal projects look like this:

EMAILS—SHORT, MEAN, AND DEMANDING

I like to send emails when I'm not in the office (which is most of the time) that send the employees spiraling. It's amazing what puts them on edge. The trick is to send emails about projects that I haven't discussed with employees. This advice is along the same lines as Spirit Tip #5 from Chapter 2: Keep Employees on Their Toes. Here are a few examples:

EMAIL EXAMPLE #1:

Dan,

You should look at these materials. What we want to accomplish here is to edit together a video for buyers / distributors that helps them understand why our protagonist is the ambassador for the show. Work with Juan to get a cut put together ASAP.

EMAIL EXAMPLE #2:

Sabrina,

Where are you with this RFP?

EMAIL EXAMPLE #3:

Rick,

This is not what I asked for. Let's set a call to discuss . . .

There's a strength and determination in these emails that are unmatched. These emails have:

1. No adjectives. Nothing beyond articles and possessives.
2. No signatures. This makes employees think that I am unhappy. It also makes it seem that I am not finished with my thought—that I'm still thinking about it.
3. No details. How long is the video? When is it due? When should we set a call? My employees need to figure it out or try to reach me.

My employees often send me documents to correct, edit, or review. When reviewing documents, it's important to email each individual correction. For example, Meghan sends me documents about "process, format, and flow." I think she visited China once and got too happy with the feng shui stuff. What does a streamlined document mean, anyways? It's not trying to swim or fly.

Meghan is like a puppy: eager and scatter-brained. She can lose things sometimes, so as I read a document she's sent me, I email her with every edit I make. Once, I sent her forty emails in thirty minutes. This way, she doesn't lose track. She usually sends me a revised version after my first few edits, but I just leave her in radio silence. I never respond to her revision until I've finished correcting the first draft. She's a bit impetuous, and she needs to become a little more tortoise-like to win the race for my approval.

EXPECTATIONS—GREAT

I don't ask for much. I pay my employees, and for that I expect them to work. So, when Sabrina doesn't answer my email on the Saturday of Memorial Day weekend, I know that she's not dedicated. She doesn't have what it takes to have what I've got. She's answered emails on the weekends before, but she didn't answer this one. Shame. I thought she was a good one. Guess not. I purposefully email over weekends and call on week-nights. I want my employees to know that they're under my control. Especially managers—they should know that they're on call. And it's a great expectation because they're only sup-posed to work forty hours a week. By having them cater to my every whim, I can get twice as much work out of them for the same amount of money as I could get from someone with more self-respect.

EMPLOYEE INTERACTION—INADVISABLE

When I'm in the office, I have the displeasure of speaking to my employees. I have an office at the studio. It's all glass and faces the exit so that I can still keep an eye on when my employees come and go. My biggest pet peeve is when my employees see me in my office and walk in and talk to me. They ask me about my day or how I'm doing. Can't they see that I'm working? They're like dogs that need affection, but that's not my job.

When I do interact with my employees, I engage them within an environment that I can control, but lets them feel like they have the power. For example, I try to get my employees' opinions on what they think they know. It's usually about stuff I don't care about, like "theories" and "trends." Recently, I started a debate about the difference between "corporate social responsibility" and "creating shared value." Blood was almost shed. I put on my dog costume. It was great, like a game show hosted by a furry animal.

As I've said before, I put the fear of God in my employees, which also makes them my yes-guys and yes-gals. But every once in a while, I have employees tell me how they really feel and even give me advice for how they think I should run my business. Their candor makes me gag. Literally. If a peon criticizes me, I puke. And that I will not tolerate. What they fail to see is that it's my business, which means that I'm always right. By the mere existence of my business, I'm correct. When Sabrina was first hired, she would send me long emails of why I shouldn't purchase certain assets and blah blah blah because it was an unnecessary expense and didn't serve a function for the business. I told her, "If I approve it, then it's correct." Ever since, she's not pushed back on any of my requests.

THE APPEARANCE
OF WORK BEING DONE
IS MORE
IMPORTANT
THAN
ACTUAL
WORK
BEING DONE

CHAPTER 4

HUMAN RESOURCES (HR)

If you wanna get your point across, you gotta cuss.
—Easy E

HR IS A NECESSARY EVIL in the business world. HR only exists because employees are pussies, and the government wants its nose up my ass.

RECRUITING

Process, process, blah, blah, blah. My project manager Meghan is also responsible for recruiting. She has flow charts for every goddamn thing around the office—even for tossing food or recycling paper.

> Side note: I am a huge supporter of the green movement. Green makes the world go round, and the more green, the better. The more the world resembles money, the more society will stay on task for the only important commodity that exists: perceived value.

So, "RACI-Chart"* Meghan always pushes me to get Dan, our creative director, to assist with hiring artists. She wants him to write job descriptions and review resumes. Why? That's a waste of his time. He should just be making art. I'm the only one that needs to determine who fits on what Meghan calls the "team." By the way, the word *fit* is overrated. I don't want people to "fit." I want them to disappear into the business eco-system that I've crafted with my mind's eye.

Meghan is also persistent about not posting a job unless I am seriously looking to fill the position immediately. Some-times I see that she doesn't post a job right away. This negates the work I do in creating the job description.

> Side note: To write a job description, I copy and paste other similar job descriptions that I've found together into one document. I don't spend too much time on it, because job descriptions are overrated, and I can make any job description of someone else's work for my business.

My goal is to hire the best person. That person does not have to be the same person for the job that I was originally looking for. As long as I hire someone that's young and hungry that I can manipulate, then that is the right person. Most of the time I tell someone that their job will be one thing, and it turns out to be a complete 180. That's why I hired Rick, with a master's degree in computer science. I told him I wanted the studio

---

* RACI Chart: A common type of responsibility matrix that uses responsible, accountable, consult, and inform statuses to define the involvement of stake-holders in project activities.

Project Management Institute, *A guide to the project management body of knowledge (PMBOK® guide), 6th ed.* (Newtown Square, PA: Project Manage-ment Institute, 2017), 718.

to build an animation pipeline with full integration between softwares. And he accepted the position. But that's not what I was going to have him do at all. Always tell the best candidates what they want to hear about a job they're interested in. Then, once you hire them, you can make them do whatever you want. Now, he works on the website by using some drag-and-drop website builder. No HTML coding required.

Back to Meghan not posting jobs when I ask her to. She says that posting jobs and not returning emails, phone calls, or interviews gives the company a poor reputation in the community. I told her that I was the company's community reputation and that accumulating resumes is a business strategy. If no one teaches her, then who will? Sometimes I care about my employees a little too much.

INTERVIEWS

I should be able to ask prospective employees whatever I want in an interview. After all, I don't want nutjobs working here and scaring my other employees. If I want to ask what a girl's into, then I should be able to. Don't worry, I didn't. I hired her, and *then* asked her if she was gay or straight.

A NOTE ON PROCESS

One day, I hired an intern on the spot and told her she could start that day. I hope that teaches Meghan that process is mere bureaucracy that impedes "making money moves."*

---

* "Bodak Yellow," featuring Kodak Black, Spotify, Track 4 on Cardi B, Invasion of Privacy, Atlantic Records, 2017.

A NEW EMPLOYEE'S FIRST DAY

An employee's first day should be as chaotic and unplanned as possible, like a stress test. I never show up to the office on an employee's first day, but I do watch via spy camera. Many times, I hire people and tell no one. Then when they walk in, I run to my computer and email Meghan and Sabrina telling them that there's a new employee. When this happens, they typically pour themselves coffee and run around. Sometimes it's better than TV.

DISCIPLINARY ACTION POLICY

When it comes time to discipline an employee (and that time always comes for every employee), I tell another employee to tell the disciplined employee what they did wrong and what their punishment is. For example, if Meghan screws up (which she often does), then I tell Sabrina to tell Meghan that she screwed up and that a letter is going in her file. Three letters, and the employee is out. Just like baseball. This policy demonstrates three important lessons: 1) I do not tolerate mistakes, 2) I never give my employees direct feedback, because this indicates that I care too much about them, and 3) I always want my employees to know that I talk about their poor work with other employees.

FIRING EMPLOYEES

"I hate firing employees." That's what you need your employees to think you feel. I actually enjoy firing employees, but not

for the reason you think. No, I'm not some vicious capitalist pummeling through people. I also don't call it "firing." I
"let my people go." It means that they weren't good enough to
make the cut. And like all things you use the *love* word with,
you have to let them go, or they'll drag you down with them.

I make it a point to hint that I might let an employee go.
If I schedule a meeting with an employee on a Friday at 5:30
p.m., then that employee will know that we're going to have a
serious talk. I like to do these meetings towards the end of the
business day because it's important that other employees don't
get to say goodbye. An employee is typically pissed when I let
them go, so it's best they don't spread their bad attitude to the
rest of the clan. And then, after they leave, I go to a bar for
happy hour.

The best part of teasing that I'll let someone go? It makes
your employees fear you, and that's true power.

"HOLIDAY" PARTY

It's a Christmas party. Grow up, people. My employees don't
care. I've asked if it offended anyone, and they didn't say anything. I spent a day on my laptop in the kitchen. For every
employee that came in, I asked them if they thought we
should celebrate Hanukkah instead of Christmas after we've
been having a Christmas party for five years. No one said yes.

HALLOWEEN PARTY

This is one of my favorite staff events. Every year, I pay for my
employees to have a staff Halloween party. It's the only staff

HR thing I can really get into. I introduce it every year in September at an all-staff meeting. It goes like this:

Me: "Good news. I've decided that we're going to have a staff Halloween party this year."

I pause for excitement. The new hires clap and giggle. The employees that have been on staff for a few years sigh or bow their heads.

Me: "We are going to have finger foods catered in and a mini liquor bar for the first two hours. And I want you all to wear a costume."

The new hires lose their cool.

Amy: "I'm going to dress up like Ang the avatar."

Meredith: "I'm going as Princess Caroline from *BoJack Horseman*."

> Side Note: Did I mention that I hire mostly women? Oh yeah, they cost less and do more work. Plus, they keep the place cleaner and look more attractive. I'm a feminist because I hire women.

Bryan sits in a corner. He looks down at his crossed legs. He bites his lips. He's been here a while.

Bryan: "Are you going to show up this time?"

I pause. He's testing me.

Me: "Yeah. I'll try. I'm a busy guy, Bryan. Besides, I just want you to be able to cut loose and have fun."

Bryan: "Sure. I just—it's just . . ."

Me: "What?"

Bryan: "It's weird to have the bar right in front of the camera up front here. It just feels like we're being watched. It's hard to cut loose when you've got Big Brother at a party."

Me: "I want people to drink as much as they want. Just

don't break anything. Understood?"

Bryan: "Yeah, okay."

Me: "Anyone have any other problems? Okay, wear your costumes. The furrier, the better."

Maggie: "I don't have anything furry. Is fuzzy okay?"

Me: "Fuzzy is perfect."

Of course, I don't show up to the party, and the bar is angled toward the spy camera. I sit, watch, and drink in my costume from my own home.

BATHROOM POLICY

I have IBS, and I'm not ashamed of it. I just don't usually talk about it. Many Americans are in a constant state of surviving IBS. So, when I do show up to the office, sometimes I take a shit. As anyone else with IBS knows, it's difficult to control where the shit flies. When I shit, I explode. And flushing doesn't flush all the shit all the time, especially when there's shit on the sides of the bowl.

There is one men's bathroom in my facility. One bathroom, one stall, and two urinals. One urinal doesn't work, because it holds pee in the catch and stinks up the place. If I see a guy stick his prick near that one, I slap it.

I heard through the spy camera that employees are talking amongst themselves to find out who the shitter is. What they do know is that the shitter itself is only dirty when I visit. So at the next all-staff a month later, I brought it up.

> Side Note: It's important to have staff meetings few and far between. The less that employees get to know each other, the more power I wield. If they're friends, they'll revolt.

I told them they have to respect the space.

Me: "If you make a mess, you have to clean it up. That goes for the dishes, the trash, and the bathroom. If you can't keep the bathroom clean, then it begs the question: 'Do you want to be here?'"

Later, on the camera (because I got the hell out of there after the meeting), I saw Bryan with gloves, wipes, and cleaner headed toward the bathroom. He was going to clean my shit.

One day I was pissing in the urinal, talking to myself, when Rick walked in. My dick was leaking a little on the floor, and we made eye contact.

From the camera feed at the front desk:

Meghan: "I heard from some of the guys that they think he's [that's me] dirtying the bathroom."

Sabrina: "What do you mean by 'dirtying'?"

Meghan: "They said he shits up the sides of the bowl and leaves it there to crust."

It's a lot of fun to watch your employees talk about your shit. That's ultimate power. If you can do that, then you can do anything. I took a play out of Bobby's Knight's playbook: show your players your shit.* Literally.

Additional camera feed later that day:

Sabrina: "Rick, I heard that he [that's me] shits up the toilet?"

Rick: "Yeah!"

Sabrina: "Why didn't anyone say anything?"

---

* Bob Knight coached Indiana University basketball from 1971–2000. He allegedly wiped himself and showed it to players to demonstrate how they were playing: "Former Players Break Silence About Bobby Knight; Indianians Rally Around Coach," CNN Transcripts, CNN, published 2001, http://transcripts. cnn.com/TRANSCRIPTS/0003/15/nsst.00.html.

Rick: "He also pisses on the floor."

Sabrina: "Intentionally?"

Rick: "I don't know. I've seen him. You know. Like I've SEEN him."

Sabrina: "Yeah."

Rick: "When he pees, he gestures and talks to himself."

Studies show that talking to myself is a sign of intelligence.*
I guess that's something Rick will never understand.

My employees can be persistent: Sabrina put up a sign in the bathroom that asks everyone to "Please Clean Up After Yourself." You'd think they'd know by now that whatever rules or policies they make don't apply to me.

LUNCH POLICY

My employees get an hour of unpaid lunch a day. Generous, I know. I usually send emails right before lunch and ask for something immediately. This means that employees end up working through lunch. And they wouldn't dare leave early, because they know I'm watching them through the camera. It's a great way to get more work out of my employees. When I'm in the office, I stick around to get a free lunch. Usually, my employees walk to a market or a coffee shop and bring the food back to the office. When I see one of them walking on their way out for lunch, I ask to join them. This is great because they can't say no. In the five years that I've had my company, no one has said no to me. And they shouldn't. The

---

* Paul Ratner, "Talking to Yourself Out Loud May Be a Sign of Higher Intelligence, Find Researchers," Big Think, May 10, 2017, https://bigthink.com/paul-ratner/ why-talking-to-yourself-out-loud-might-be-just-what-your-brain-needs.

best part is that I don't pay. I slide in with my order before they can get their wallets out. My employees are proud to thank me for their work. My favorite lunch is when I ask them to pick something up for me, and I take it on my way out of the office.

SALARIES

I pay my employees way below the going market value. This is because I mostly hire recent female college graduates that are thankful to have a job. I make it a rule to pay all my employees 20 percent below the going market rate, and I pay women 15 percent below that. The key to paying low wages is opening a shop in an industry that is geographically isolated. Because my company is in the animation industry and is located in the Midwest, animators that live here are merely happy to work and are trying to build their portfolios. It's a win-win, really. If I were to do it again, I would open a fishing business in the Sonoran.

OVERTIME

I make sure that all of my employees are full-time nonexempt. It's the only way that I get enough work out of them. And every single one of them is expected to be on call 24-7. Especially managers. I expect my managers to answer my every call, text, and email immediately. If I email Sabrina and she doesn't respond within ten minutes, I call her. It's just good oversight. I can't trust her to do things without my prodding her. She's not that experienced. She's been pissing me off lately, though. She answered only one of my emails while she was on vacation. She told me she was going on a cruise or something. I told her on the last Zoom call that I had with her that I needed her to be on call during her vacation. The key to getting the most out of your employees is not asking, it's telling. Fear is always more powerful than the alternative. Besides, if employees fear you, then they respect you.

What's even better about having nonexempt employees is that I do not have to pay them for overtime. I don't even offer comp time. This is key to setting up any business. Make your employees know that their lives are your business.

SICK DAYS

All employees must report to work unless they're in the hospital. If they're in the hospital, then they have to call me and tell me what happened and how long they'll be there.

If I see an employee come to work sick when I'm in the office, I send them home immediately. I don't want them germing up the place while I'm there. How dare they come in and spread germs. Their toxicity is infectious.

HOLIDAYS AND VACATION TIME

After this past Christmas, I had Sabrina implement a new vacation policy to start at the beginning of the calendar year. The new policy is that all employees get five days of vacation (I'm generous, I know).

> Side Note: I love America. One of the things I love most about America is that there is no federally mandated holiday or vacation time that employers have to provide. It's a joy to tell my employees during staff meetings that

| they could have none, but I give them five.

All employees get five days of vacation. Everyone took it at Christmas the following year. I called Sabrina, who was the only person who didn't use her days during Christmas (she went on that cruise and didn't answer my emails right away). I told her that I could no longer allow all the employees to take off during the holiday. I just can't NOT have employees in the office. **The appearance of work being done is more important than actual work being done.** Per my request, she wrote up a policy that states 1) only one employee may take vacation at a time and 2) no employee is permitted to use their vacation days to extend their holiday time off. They already get Christmas Day off—that should be plenty.

ATTENDANCE

Employees must sign in promptly at 9:00 a.m. and not a minute later. Every morning, I watch employees stumble into the building. If I see anyone enter after 9:00 a.m., they immediately get a phone call from me. These days, you have to threaten employees to show up on time. I fired an employee for showing up at 9:38 a.m. His excuse was that he was in a car accident. I asked Sabrina to go check out his car and send me a picture. In fact, he was in an accident, but I can't have my employees thinking it's okay to show up to work late.

In addition to clocking in promptly at 9:00 a.m., employees must also sign out at 6:00 p.m. Some of them stay later, and I despise that. I hate overachievers. Besides, I don't want people hanging out after business hours. What are they doing in there? They usually stand in a place where I can't see them from my spy camera. I've told them in staff meetings to get the hell out. They keep telling me that they start rendering* at the end of the day and wait a while before they leave to make sure that the computer doesn't crash. My computers don't crash. I make sure Rick knows that.

If I see that an employee doesn't abide by my clock-in and clock-out rules, then I email them when they're at home even more. If an employee pisses me off, I make sure I pester them with more work.

WORK FROM HOME

There is no working from home. Don't let your employees do it.

PET POLICY

Absolutely no pets. I went into an office with dogs once. There was shit everywhere. If anyone is going to take a shit on the floor, it's going to be me.

PROTECTED STATUSES

Federal and state governments only enact laws to protect the type of people that have complained enough to get either an amendment out of the Constitution or a ruling from the Supreme Court.

---

* Rendering is the process of generating a photorealistic or non-photorealistic image from a 2D or 3D model by means of a computer program. "Rendering (computer graphics)," Wikipedia, Wikipedia, last modified November 16 2020, https://en.wikipedia.org/wiki/Rendering_(computer_graphics).

It's hard to find employees that don't make a federal case about every goddamn thing nowadays. These kids think they live in a world where working for a "good" person is a worker's right. My employees got up my ass recently for approving a piece of artwork to send to a commercial client. I'm in the animation industry—which is why I can ask my artists to make anything I want, and it will be interpreted how I say it will be interpreted. If I tell them to model a turd, I want to see that turd, and I will interpret it as a fucking masterpiece. I can't remember what the ad was for, but it was a collage of items with one thing in the middle. I asked the artist to move a few things around, and they thought it was offensive. How can having a gun point in the direction of a Black guy be offensive? The gun isn't even pointed "at" him: it's only pointed in his direction. Sometimes I think that these kids are so quick to complain about everything. None of them are even Black! I don't know what you would call Juan. I think he may be from Mexico?

SOCIAL MEDIA POLICY

Using cameras to spy on my employees at work is not enough. And unfortunately, it takes a lot more effort to be aware of your employees' every move than I would prefer to exert. But it's my business, and I need to know what my employees are doing at all times. So, I look them up on social media. I recently saw that Juan kept sharing paintings he created on his Instagram. One thing I will not tolerate is passing off work that was done for me as work that my employees did themselves. So, I called Meghan.

Me: "Meghan, I see that Juan and a few others are posting art on social media. Something must be done about this."

Meghan: "I'm sorry. What's the problem?"

Me: "They can't twit art created in my studio online. That's my property."

Meghan: "Juan works on his own art at home and posts that. And did you mean tweet?"

Me: "How can he prove that?"

Meghan: "Prove that he makes art in his own time at his house?"

Me: "Yeah."

I try to back my employees into a corner of insanity so that they don't know how to respond. If they can't reason with me, then they can't argue with me. Of course, after this conversation, I brought up posting art in the all-staff.

Juan: "You can't tell us what we can or cannot post on our personal social media accounts."

Me: "When it's my property, I can."

Juan: "I don't post your property, man."

Me: "Just don't do it."

And that's that. Works every time. Now he doesn't post any more art on Instagram. At least, not on the account he was posting on . . . I should see if he has any other accounts.

I also saw that my employees are very open with their political views on social media. Whatever happened to the good old days when we all nodded and smiled at each other? As long as the news doesn't affect me, I'm cool as a cucumber. Knowing the kids these days, they would probably say that saying "cool as a cucumber" is transphobic or something.

I can't have my employees being politically active on the

twits. Especially when they twit every five minutes. Every five minutes? How can my employee get any work done if they twit every five minutes? And it takes more time out of my day if I have to wait to read what an employee twits every five minutes. I don't care how much work is getting done: no one can twit every five minutes, even if there are protests in the streets. So, I asked Sabrina to write up a social media policy to stick in the Handbook. She sent me some long memo about how I can't tell people what they can or cannot post using social media. I just ignored her. What the hell does she know anyways? I skimmed her book-length email. She kept mentioning the National Labor Relations Act and federal rulings of other social media policies. Doesn't she know that OSHA and other federal agencies like the NLRB are a bunch of pussies? Those organizations' only job is to stifle creative businesses like mine. So, I ignored her essay. Next day, at the end of the day, she quit. I went back and read the last bit of her email: it said if she didn't hear back that she would quit. Damn girl didn't give me a chance to fire her.

INTERNAL MEETINGS

Meetings happen with the people I say they will happen with. I don't want some random person to be a part of a conversation that I didn't say they were permitted to be privy to. Meghan is the worst at this. She used to set meetings with every employee that she thought had to be involved in the conversation. I would tell her that we needed a meeting with her and I to discuss tech. And then Rick would show up to the meeting. Even though I asked Rick a few questions during the meeting, I told Sabrina to tell Meghan that I wasn't happy that Rick showed up to the meeting. Now, Meghan asks me whom she should invite to meetings. I never respond to those emails. It's her job to set meetings, not mine.

CLIENT-FACING MEETINGS

It's important to show my employees and my guests that both groups are in the studio because of me. This makes both groups look up to me and seek my direction. When I meet clients, I give them a tour of the facility. Of course, I give my employees no heads-up, because this is a drill. What if we have the governor visit the facility? There will definitely be no heads-up then. Typically, I show up thirty minutes before visitors are due to arrive, and I plod through the building shouting at people to get ready. Then, Rick and I get into it, because I tell him to play an animation clip that I deleted a few years ago. He needs to be reminded that I'm the man and he's the peon.

All my employees are at their stations, and the guests arrive. I walk them through each room one by one. Even if a room is empty, my guests have to see the entire space. Just as bigger is better, square footage measures the man.

Bryan's station is the postproduction compositing and color station. I make sure that I'm honest with my guests. After Bryan shows some animation, I tell them that he's not actually a colorist or compositor; he's just a poser.

After the tour, I heard my employees complaining about this comment. They said it was mean and humiliating to Bryan. But he didn't say anything to me, so I guess it didn't bother him. Even if it did bother him and he told me about it,

I would tell him that in business it's necessary to be upfront with people. Surely, he would respect that.

BUSINESS EXPENSES

It's my business, and I am above the rules. Expense policies apply to employees spending my money. I don't need rules to dictate how I spend my own company's funds. The most genius expenses I debit* are when I'm "traveling for work."

> Side Note: I don't work on business trips. I meet with people and gab. I do deals during *Monday Night Football* while nacho cheese runs down my chin.

Most recently, I visited an animation studio in Montreal. I pretended that I was going to hire the studio for an animated feature film, but all I was really doing was studying how my studio could copy how they do business. To make the trip seem innocent, I brought my son with me. My son is in high school, and he's a little weird (he freaks me out actually, and I think he could be a serial killer one day). But the kid is a genius and an autodidact. My rule of thumb is that a "business" trip is a family trip. My employees were pretty pissed when they found out that I took my son to Montreal instead of Dan. I didn't take Dan because I was going on a business trip for vacation. Besides, my business is none of my employees' business.

Recently, the government gave my company economic relief funds for a tornado that pummeled through the area. It didn't do any damage to my facility, but I told Sabrina to apply

---

* In accounting, debits are funds that leave a bank account, and credits are funds that go into a bank account.

for the funds anyways. And we got the disbursement as I had predicted. Apparently, there are special rules for how the government allows businesses to spend the money: a certain percentage has to be used for payroll, and a certain percentage has to be used for rent and utilities. I was bummed that the government didn't allow the funds to be used for payments on loan interest (wouldn't it be great if the government paid my business to pay me?). I already do that with my taxes. I guess I can't triple dip old Uncle Sam . . . yet. I have a friend in the Senate that I can pay to submit a bill. Anyways, Sabrina sent me a spreadsheet that showed that there had to be an increase in spending on payroll or else my company would have to return the money or pay interest on it as a loan. I couldn't return the money because that would be in violation of the two most important rules in business. They are:

1.   Never return money.

2.   Lie your ass off.

So, I called Sabrina.

Me: "I have to spend nine grand in a month and a half on payroll?"

Sabrina: "Yes, we could temporarily increase everyone's salaries as a bonus for that time period and decrease them again after the money is spent."

Me: "We're going to hire my son. He'll be part-time. Figure out whatever hourly rate it is to spend the nine grand."

Sheer genius. Your taxpayer dollars went straight to my son. If that doesn't make me a motherfucking king, I don't know what does.

CHAPTER 5

NAME DROP TO SHOW WHO'S BOSS

You either evolve or you disappear.
—*Tupac Shakur*

I RAN INTO Tripp Welborne from back in my Michigan days. He was working at some bank and helping me move my money around. It must have been awkward for him.

I email John Legend regularly; in fact, I emailed John Legend before John Legend was John Legend. John Legend.

I ran into Cyndi Lauper at a pool party in Kaui. She was covered in clothes, and you could barely tell it was her.

Klaus Bedault takes me out to dinner every time I go to LA. He still owes me.

Lin Manuel Girly Name is a toolbox. He saw me at a film festival wrap party and completely ignored me. He knew who I was.

Wayne Gretzky stepped on my hand at an orgy. He said, "He misses every step he doesn't take." So, I guess he meant to step on my hand. He's also a toolbox.

I could go on, but I don't care about impressing my readers that much.

INDUSTRY IS IRRELEVANT TO A COMPANY'S BUSINESS STRATEGY

CHAPTER 6

STRATEGY

If you die in an elevator, make sure you press the up button.
—*50 Cent*

THIS WOULDN'T BE A business how-to-be-successful-like-me book if I didn't talk about some economic theory. It'll be quick but painful—like a woman's first time. Everyone in management and economics is always talking about this Michael Porter guy. Ever since the nineties, he's the deity of strategy. It's all nonsense. Every time you hear the name Michael Porter, plug your ears and go "la, la, la" to save yourself the trouble of weeding through the bullshit.

This Porter dude is some Harvard hot-to-trot shot that wants everyone across the globe to hold hands and sing "Kumbaya." If he had it his way, all businesses would be like the ice cream label Ben & Jerry's: gay and sweet. He jeopardizes businesses' ability to make money because he has completely undermined the definition of business strategy. Never trust a guy that tells you he knows everything unless that guy is me. Porter uses words like *fit* and *forces*. The last time I heard those words, I was watching *Star Wars*, and I don't think the Jedi know how to turn a profit.

Some of the most dangerous things that Porter has said are that efficiency isn't strategy and that strategy means saying no to customers.* Has this guy never worked a day in his life? I say this to warn you again: plug your goddamn ears. People like him should be locked away in jail. Businesses fail when they turn customers away. Admittedly, that's why my company's services are an inch deep and a mile wide. We need to be able to do whatever the customer wants, because the customer is always right. I'm currently talking to a prospective client right now that wants us to create an escape room. I say no problem. I'll source cheap labor and skim 20 percent off the top for my company to pay interest on its loans from me.

Efficiency is the only means by which a business can rake in the cash. That's why I make my business try new things. How am I supposed to know what my business can do if it doesn't branch out? Business is like sex. The more you do it, the better you get. And the more freaky, the more interesting. I tried this new thing recently—all I'll say is, Fuzzy Wuzzy was my bear.

Porter talks about company strategy within a company's industry. **Industry is irrelevant to a company's business strategy.** You're either good at business or you're not. Business is like football: it doesn't matter where you play, it's how you win. But Porter has a list. Something he calls his "Five Forces"† to gauge strategy within an industry. I've listed them

---

* Michael E. Porter, "What is Strategy?" *Harvard Business Review* 74, no. 6 (November–December 1996): 61–78

† Michael E. Porter, "The Five Competitive Forces That Shape Strategy," Special

below so I can beat up on them:

PORTER'S FIVE FORCES

1. Competition in the industry
2. Potential of new entrants into the industry
3. Power of suppliers
4. Power of buyers
5. Threat of substitute buyers

Half of this stuff, I don't even know what it means. Porter seems to be one prick getting high off mind games. The next time some economist mentions the Five Forces at a party to make himself seem smart, go by the chart below.

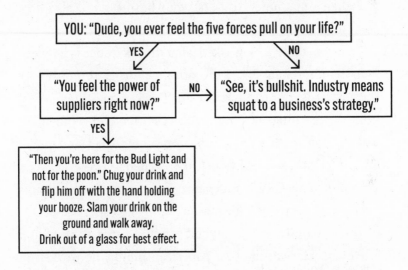

I have my own list of trade secrets that are NOT meant to trick you—they actually define strategy. The big secret to running a successful business is what I call Boondoggleness. Because my business is a boondoggle, I've included the Five

Factors of Boondoggleness.

FIVE FACTORS OF BOONDOGGLENESS

1. Send emails every three minutes.
2. Schedule surprise meetings.
3. Demand answers immediately.
4. Yell at people.
5. Fire people.

If you fire people, you must replace them. I'll add a sixth (one more than Porter).

6. Hire a family member.

If you follow the five factors of boondoggleness plus one, then I guarantee you that your business will also be a boondoggle.

I am constantly being asked what the difference is between social entrepreneurship and corporate social responsibility. The answer is: I don't fucking care. This is a question derived from the teachings of Porter. Forget Porter. He's a blowhard that's trying to take money out of your pocket and put it toward "creating shared value," abbreviated as CSV.*

> Side note: CSV is a filename. It stands for "cash screams virility." CSV is a file masquerading as a spreadsheet.

The economist that everybody should listen to is Milton Friedman. Like all the best American minds, he worked in the Midwest—at the University of Chicago in the seventies. He allowed businesses to flourish by preaching the idea that a business's number one priority is maximizing shareholder

---

* Porter, Michael E. and Kramer, Mark R. "Creating Shared Value." *Harvard Business Review*, Reprint R1101C, Jan.–Feb. 2011, pp. 1–17.

Michael E. Porter., Mark R. Kramer, and Jane Nelson, "Creating Shared Value: Connecting Business, Societal Value and Opportunity." FSG, 2011.

wealth. And he damned anyone who used the phrase "corporate social responsibility."* Simply put, a corporation's social
responsibility is to make as much money as it can. Praise
Friedman. If there were a church of Friedman, I'd convert.
Hell, I'd be gay for that guy. And that's why I do the things I
do: all in the name of making money. That's why any business
worth its salt (especially salt businesses) have one goal: make
the moola for the owners. I would be failing my employees if
I didn't pay them as little as I do to make more money for me.
I would be violating the foundation of economic theory in the
US of A if I didn't make as much money for me as I possibly
could. That's why I do what I can to improve the economy:
I've been known to skip out on paying people their contracts
or stealing IP from folks and then suing them for stealing it
from me. I am improving every American's well-being every
time I add a dollar to my bank account. That's why poor
people should shut up.

Porter also talks about companies being a leader in an
industry by changing the industry with an understanding of
the five forces. But that's not the point of business. A business's
goal is to make as much money as possible for the owners /
/ boondogglers / whatever. He also says that "an improved
industry structure is a public good."† Again, the best public
good I can do is make money. I can't make money by improving an industry and giving information to my competitors.
The best "good" I can do is annihilating an industry

---

* Milton Friedman, "The Social Responsibility of Business is to Increase its
Profits," *New York Times*, September 13, 1970.
† Michael E. Porter, "The Five Competitive Forces That Shape Strategy," Special
Issue on HBS Centennial, *Harvard Business Review* 86, no. 1 (January 2008):
78–93.

by being the industry. This is why monopolies are crucial to the American economy, and why the game Monopoly should be a mandatory game for all kids in grade school. I need to undermine the animation industry so that I am king and owner of all animation. Every morning I wake up, look myself in the mirror, and say: "I am king shit of fuck mountain. Why would you fuck with me?"

> Side Note: This is a direct quote from a sketch called "Swear to God" on HBO's *Mr. Show* by Bob Odenkirk and David Cross from the nineties. Typically, I don't credit other people for their work, but this statement is a perfect description of me.

Milton Friedman has this outstanding lecture called "I, Pencil" about . . . pencils. If you didn't see that coming, then you're a moron and don't tell anyone you read this book. You don't need to watch Friedman's talk online because I'm going to describe it to you here. He shows the future, dominated by pencils. Pencils seem pleasant until one guy (he's Black) figures out that pencils are trying to take over the world. Then he kills a bunch of pencils with pencils. It's pretty great and somehow manages to show that no one knows how to make a pencil.

Before I crush Porter anymore, let me first sidestep. There are other people championing this idea of "creating shared value." Be careful. They will steal your money. Since 2007, there's been this movement called the B Corp (think bad corp) movement. It's founded by the group of guys that used to own AND1 before they sold out for the big bucks. Now they're trying to prevent others from starting a business and selling it above its actual value like they did. B Corp is a group that dupes businesses into drinking its hippie juice to achieve peace, love, and the uh-oh word—sustainability. B Corp has a certification process for these "businesses" in which they fill out a form based upon what they do to see if it passes the hippie test. If a "business" receives an 80, it's a Certified B Corp, AKA, hippie official. Then, the newly-identified hippie companies can slap a B on their products. Woo hoo. It reminds me of that one movie with Jason Bateman and another guy (he's Black) that's bad at being a superhero. Jason Bateman's pussy-ass character tries to sell heart labels to companies as a "corporate social responsibility" ploy. But nobody buys it. **If it doesn't work in the movies, it doesn't work in real life.**

IF IT DOESN'T WORK IN THE MOVIES IT DOESN'T WORK IN REAL LIFE

I think it's great that these "for-profit businesses" waste their time smoking a peace pipe and dreaming of a tomorrow that they would prefer. That just leaves more room for me to bust some balls.

BUSTED BALL #1: THE TRIPLE-BOTTOM LINE

B Corp is a proponent of the triple-bottom line (people, planet, profit). It's the type of bullshit that forces business costs to increase due to paying employees a "living wage" and doing business while keeping the uh-oh word* in mind (things like "responsibly" sourcing materials and producing and distributing "ethical" products). This forces businesses into making higher-end products to sell at a higher price point. That makes me the only person thinking about poor people. You gotta swindle the shit out of your suppliers and vendors to sell cheap products for the folks that aren't smart enough to make as much money as me. And the companies that try to be good for goodness's sake? They go out of business. Best example in my industry: Rhythm & Hues.†

---

* The uh-oh word is sustainability.

† Rhythm & Hues started as a company that put their employees first. Its founder eventually made dubious investments. The company filed for bankruptcy three months after winning an Academy Award for Visual Effects for *Life of Pi*.

See: David Y. Choi and Edmund R. Gray, "Socially Responsible Entrepreneurs: What Do They Do to Create and Build Their Companies?" *Business Horizons* 51 (2008): 341-352.

Eriq Gardner, "Former Rhythm & Hues Owners Sued for Having 'Pillaged' Oscar-Winning VFX House," *Hollywood Reporter*, February 16, 2015, https://www.hollywoodreporter.com/thr-esq/rhythm-hues-owners-sued-having-773839.

There's even a handbook for this stuff written by a guy with the last name of Honeyman. He says "B Corps matter because they accelerate the evolution of capitalism."* Doesn't he know that God created capitalism? No evolution required. This whole shared value/B Corp mumbo jumbo is a cult. Listen to the nonsense for very long, and soon you'll wind up with an organic cotton Fair Trade Certified™ gag in your mouth, getting dragged to some sheik yurt by a lake where you'll never be heard from again. I'll list a few companies that are B Corps so you know to avoid them and that scenario:

1. Ben & Jerry's
2. Seventh Generation
3. Patagonia
4. Etsy
5. Cabot Creamery
6. New Belgium Brewing Company

BUSTED BALL #2: "SUSTAINABLE" SUPPLY CHAINS

I would be remiss if I didn't deride the high and mighty, ever-so-green, hippie people at Patagonia. Founder Yvon Chouinard's hippie dippie book about Patagonia is called *Let My People Go Surfing*. What if they don't want to? Sounds like a bad petri dish scenario to me. Patagonia prides itself on quality and "sustainable" supply chains. **A "sustainable" supply chain is code for "so expensive that your baby-boomer mother or grandmother would shit her pants at the price tag."** As I said previously in this godforsaken chapter:

---

* Ryan Honeyman, *The B Corp Handbook: How to Use Business as a Force for Good* (San Francisco: Berrett-Koehler Publishers, Inc., 2014).

"sustainable" supply chains "responsibly" source materials to produce "ethical" products.

For example, in the '90s, Patagonia made a big deal of switching from regular, good old American industrial cotton to organic cotton. The difference is that industrial cotton is made with machines and pesticides and organic cotton is made with hippie juice and sex. Patagonia even checks how "ethical" their vendors are by visiting the plants overseas that dye materials or sew their precious waterproof undies. In his book, Chouinard even admits to discovering that a vendor of his vendor dealt in human trafficking. I say, let people conduct business their own way. I don't have to know about it. Suppliers don't have any power over me (eat it, Porter).

Plenty of other companies and start-ups are trying to source materials to achieve the uh-oh word. In their minds, it's important to give back to the planet as much as they take from it—and do this as much as possible. The goal is to let the earth live to sustain itself for as long as possible.

> Side Note: Frankly, I'll only live another forty years or so if I'm lucky, so I don't care about the state of the world after that. Yes, my son will be fine, because he'll inherit my wealth. Remember what Jesus said in the Sermon on the Mount? Only the rich shall inherit the earth.

Organizations like the US Green Building Council give out certifications called LEED—Leadership in Energy and Environmental Design, and universities now offer uh-oh word MBA concentrations and sometimes even PhDs in uh-oh. These degrees and certifications are duping poor people that are looking for a will to live into paying for education that won't get them jobs. Now that's not very responsible or ethical to me—but it is hilarious.

TO SUM STRATEGY UP

Make as much money as you can, kids. Keep your conscience clear of any "damage" you do. There will be many people that will try to put you down. Realize that they're just not as smart as you. You've read this book, and now you know to put Friedman's economic principles into practice. And when you hear the name Porter or the word uh-oh, run for the hills.

A "SUSTAINABLE" SUPPLY CHAIN

IS CODE FOR "SO EXPENSIVE THAT YOUR BABY-BOOMER MOTHER OR GRANDMOTHER WOULD SHIT HER PANTS AT THE PRICE TAG"

CHAPTER 7

MARKETING AND BUSINESS DEVELOPMENT

Florida is a kinda gold mine.
—*Vanilla Ice*

MARKETING IS JUST SEX, and sex can sell anything. The only thing that companies and their products need is a little marketing to make the big bucks. The best thing about marketing? It often keeps the little companies separated from the big ones. It takes money to make money, and marketing money buys what you spy with your little eyes. If out of sight is out of mind, then how is anyone going to buy a product that they've never even heard of? If a little business has little marketing money, chances are it will be a little amount of time before it goes out of business. Here again, the people with money get to make even more money, and the people that try to prove to themselves that they can make money end up fighting a losing battle. Long story short: the rich get richer, and the poor get poorer but learn a whole lot in the process.

Business development is sales, and sales is a do-si-do with

a prospective buyer. Just be sure not to step on the buyer's toes. If you've never danced the box step, then you're a moron or a loser without a girlfriend. If you're a woman reading this book and you've never danced the box step, that makes you a lesbian. If you're neither a man nor a woman and you're reading this book, good luck with being taken seriously in business. I would say the hardest mountain to climb in business is being taken seriously, but if you can market yourself to show your worth, then you might be able to make as much money as I have. Setbacks and all.

I KNOW THE PROBLEMS I HAVE IN MY BUSINESS BECAUSE I CAUSE MOST OF THEM

You know what goes together like a horse and carriage? No, it's not love and marriage. If you love someone, you won't marry them. It's marketing and biz dev. (Biz dev is short for business development.) You can't have one without the other, or a company might as well piss their money away on something like staff lunches and raises.

HOW TO: MARKETING

Just like there are many uses for and ways of having sex, so, too, there are many uses for and ways to market a business's products.

I know how to run my business, and I'm a ninja at business strategy. But sometimes I want to prove to people how good I am and how bad they are. So, once I hired a marketing firm to "help" with my company's strategy. Someone once told me that getting your business strategy from hiring a marketing firm is like buying milk at the hardware store. I don't care what they say; the best way to fix business problems is to market the shit out of your business. Marketing is like a scar remover for your business that makes it sexier. **I know the problems I have in my business because I cause most of them.** All the greats do. Everyone uses Steve Jobs as the god of business. That guy was a mess. So I am, too.

But, kiddos, beware. There lurks in every corporation and business school a SWOT trap. Marketing gurus love SWOT Analysis.* But it's hardly analysis at all. What these bullshit artists use to plan "strategic objectives" for "marketing plans"

---

* SWOT Analysis is a marketing tool that assesses the Strengths, Opportunities, Threats, and Weaknesses of a business.

is a chart that looks like the one below:

STRENGTHS	WEAKNESSES
OPPORTUNITIES	THREATS

Then it is the marketing guru that asks the people they're paid to help with filling out the chart. "What do you think your company's strengths are, Mr. CEO?" "What about your weaknesses, Mr. COO?" It's all pie in the sky and thumbs up your butt so-called work that these people do. It's genius that they are able to get other people to do their bullshit work for them and pay them beaucoup bucks for it.

> Side Note: Everyone that I'm related to is a genius. No one before me in my genetic line, but everyone after me, yes. It all starts at me. I am not a genius. Some people would consider me a genius, but I am not. People just think I'm a genius because I'm successful at getting other people to do really great work for me. And then I take all the credit. Now that I'm thinking about it, that must mean that people really like me if they're willing to make me look so good

Normally, I would be all for this sort of thing because it makes the American economy go round, but I've been hustled too many times by these blowhards.

What SWOT Analysis really should stand for is Suckers-

With-Only-Time. Don't fall into the SWOT trap. If someone asks you to do a SWOT Analysis, tell them to fuck off.

Unfortunately, we live in the age of digital advertising. Digital advertising is made up from all these tiny little acronyms floating around. Digital advertising can be summed up by looking at the Wordle below.

If you want to know what the acronyms mean, look them up.

HOW TO: SALES

There's the clean, and then there's the clean and jerk.* That's how I do sales. You gotta clean (lift) your clients up to your level and then bam! Jerk 'em (literally if you have to) all the way up to the top so that they are sky high and ready to buy. This is from my football days. I used to clean and jerk so hard

---

* These are two weightlifting movements.

that I would send bitches through the ceiling. That was before the #MeToo movement.

All sales are a pyramid scheme. Think about it. Sales people often sell products and services on behalf of another person or company. Anytime you give money to a sales person, there is a funnel of money that goes from the bottom to the top, whoever and wherever that may be. Just as there exists a sales funnel to push buyers through the pipeline, so also are all monies pushed backward through a similar pipeline that gives the least amount of money to the salesman that you're dealing with.

Nowadays, salesmen are told to listen to customers to build a rapport with them first in order to identify their needs. If a salesman asks you about your life, he doesn't care about you: he just wants you to trust him enough so that he can sell you a whistle. The next time you talk to a salesman, ask him questions to see how he'll respond. He'll be thrown off his programming.

Marketing and business development go hand in hand and are necessary for every business to succeed. Both come with a lot of bullshit blowhards that are trying to pull a fast one on you. If you can get by with doing the marketing and sales for your company, then that is what I recommend. I am sales and I am marketing for my company. I am the best advertisement for my company because I am a walking billboard of sex and a referral-generating machine. How do I do it? You just have to be me, and I implore you to try.

ALL SALES ARE A PYRAMID SCHEME

CHAPTER 8

PROJECT MANAGEMENT

This here is all about . . . my trials and tribulations,
my heart, my balls.
—DMX

PROJECT MANAGERS and most other businesses get bogged down in this idea that project management is difficult. Universities even offer project management as a major. The biggest joke of all is that there is an international institute dedicated to project management called the Project Management Institute. The institute has an eight-hundred-page "body of knowledge" dedicated to buzzwords like "scope" and "deliverables." The whole world is duped. The idea of merely managing a project is a complete waste of time and resources. To impress the contemporaries, I make it seem as if I have a project management system without really having one. This means that I hired Meghan to handle it and figure it out without giving her any support whatsoever, because I have better things to do.

Below is a list of processes pulled straight from the damn guide. Meghan would like for me to believe that each process not only has its processes and paperwork but also has sub-processes, sub-paperwork, sub-sub-processes, and sub-sub-paperwork.

PROJECT MANAGEMENT PROCESS*

1. Project Integration Management
2. Project Scope Management
3. Project Schedule Management
4. Project Cost Management
5. Project Quality Management
6. Project Resource Management
7. Project Communications Management
8. Project Risk Management
9. Project Procurement Management
10. Project Stakeholder Management

Ten processes for project management and this doesn't even scratch the surface of the oh-so-precious body of knowledge. When I see this, I see waste, waste, waste. There's so much time, work, people, and paperwork required to run a project according to those guidelines. There's no way a real company does this. They're all lying like I am. It's just another one of those academic monsters trying to gobble up people in the real world with their hair-brained theories and opinions.

> Side Note: Academia is overrated. I have the authority to say that because I went to grad school and teach at "the" university. Professors want the public to think that more education is better. But it's not real-world education; it's sit-on-your-ass-and-dream-fairy-tales

---

* Project Management Institute, *A guide to the project management body of knowledge: (PMBOK® guide), 6th ed.* (Newtown Square, PA: Project Management Institute, 2017), 25.

education. No one in academia actually does any work. I despise that my tax dollars go to pay those couch potatoes sitting on their fat asses, spreading poison.

Meghan truly cares about the processes behind each project. Process is her religion. It's as if she belongs to a cult. It's really quite scary.

My least favorite teachings in this project management cult boil down to three things: "scope creep," "stakeholder engagement," and "accepted deliverables." Of course, I haven't read the books these cult people read, but just like any religion, Meghan and others in the past have indirectly quoted from their religious book. Usually when I question their process, project managers like Meghan justify the process because it's "in the book of the body of knowledge that's been handed down since the Egyptians built the pyramids." It's a cult, folks. They even have church-like organizations called chapters that gather frequently to discuss the almighty body of knowledge. Recently, I found out that they even do online webinars. Some are in Spanish. Who knows what other tongues they speak in?

When Meghan hits me with a "it's in the book," I usually respond with a "what does your brain say?" That's the problem with cults: they brainwash people into doing whatever it is they want them to do blindly. Like the Manson girls. One day Meghan is going to stab me to death with a RACI chart, and I'm going to be pissed.

So, Meghan and I do a fun little do-si-do. She tries to get me to conform to her system, and I have fun dodging her efforts. Here's a few tips for fucking with the PM system:

TIPS FOR FUCKING WITH THE PM SYSTEM:

1. Never give due dates. This makes employees make their own due dates. They will always make themselves a timeline that's faster than I would have expected. It's best they push themselves.
2. Whenever due dates are given, always send your "deliverable" a day late and after "working" hours—this shows that I'm busy.
3. Communicate as little as possible. Best method: answer emails with one-word responses. If you are unsure how to respond using this method, then respond to emails as you would to texts.

According to their book, every project starts with a project charter. *"Charter"* is such a dated word that it gives me diarrhea when I hear it. Last time that word was used was during the American War for Independence. I no longer live in the thirteen original colonies; I live in the fifty nifty United States. There's no more need for charters. These project managers must have a fetish for British imperialism and colonization. They might as well sing "Rule Britannia!" Actually, it's anti-American to create a project charter. It's also important to note that international organizations like the Project Management Institute aren't American.

I'm told that the Project Charter goes hand-in-hand with the Project Scope Statement. How can an entire project boil down to one statement? I don't think it's possible. This is where "scope creep" becomes possible. "Scope creep" is like voodoo to project managers, and I'm the master at it. In order to create scope creep, I had the unfortunate plight of learning what scope means and what goes into a project scope statement. Simply put, a project scope statement is composed of four things:

PROJECT SCOPE STATEMENT

1. Project scope description
2. Project deliverables
3. Acceptance criteria
4. Project exclusions*

The whole purpose of a project scope statement and its private parts is to force business owners like me into getting less than what we deserve. It's a project manager's attempt to hold decision makers accountable to previous discussions and decisions and not let us budge. This is madness. I'm the owner, and I do what I want. "Scope creep" is the word project managers use when projects are "creeping" beyond the original "scope" of the project. I use quotes around these buzzwords because they're just fancy terms for whining about doing more work. **"Scope creep" is crucial to every business and for saving every project.** After all, it is impossible to determine all of the requirements of some projects at the beginning. For example, this escape room I'm negotiating: I don't know the first thing about escape rooms, and my employees don't, either. So how the hell is Meghan going to write a project scope statement that details all the stuff in scope?

Here's where Rick jumps in at staff meetings and starts talking about how agile he is. I told him that it was

---

* Project Management Institute, *A guide to the project management body of knowledge: (PMBOK® guide), 6th ed.* (Newtown Square, PA: Project Management Institute, 2017), 155.

inappropriate to brag about his sex life in a staff meeting. He can brag about it to anyone he likes, but I'm not wasting my time hearing about his "scrum." It's disgusting.*

Let's talk about the other buzzword that will kill my business if I don't wrangle it: stakeholder engagement. Apparently, project managers make a plan for it. I'll give you the definition straight from the horse's ass: "Stakeholder Engagement Plan: A component of the project management plan that identifies the strategies and actions required to promote productive involvement of stakeholders in project or program decision making and execution."† First, I am not a stakeholder. I don't go standing out at campsites holding stakes for other people. I think those people are actually called trail angels anyways. Second, no one is going to tell me how engaged I should or should not be in my own business. It's laughable because that's exactly what it is—my business. Where do people think the phrase "mind your own business" came from?

What I'm trying to get at is that, in general, project managers are hypocrites. These project managers are the face of highly detailed, socially conscious, and fiscally responsible leaders for projects within an organization. Yet they waste so

---

* "Agile project management is an iterative approach to project management which allows you to break large projects down into more manageable tasks tackled in short iterations or sprints. This enables your team to adapt to change quickly and deliver work fast. Scrum is a type of agile methodology."
"What Is Agile Project Management?" Agile Project Management, Workfront, accessed October 28, 2020, https://www.workfront.com/project-management/methodologies/agile

† Project Management Institute, *A guide to the project management body of knowledge: (PMBOK® guide), 6th ed.* (Newtown Square, PA: Project Management Institute, 2017), 723.

much ink and paper on all these plans, charts, and charters that I can't help but acknowledge that they're liars and thieves. I've met a real project manager (Meghan is not a real one yet. She's barely out of business school.) They're nuts about office supplies. If you ever see one, hide your pens, hide your notebooks, and hide your highlighters. Little known fact: Milton Friedman's "I, Pencil"* speech was actually about project managers changing from humans to pencils and trying to take over the world.

"SCOPE CREEP" IS CRUCIAL TO EVERY BUSINESS AND FOR SAVING EVERY PROJECT

Last but not least, let me speak to this notion of "accepted deliverables." Again, most of the work that my employees do, they do for me. So, I am the person, the "stakeholder" if your dumb ass cares, to "accept" the "deliverable." Again, these are

---

* Milton Friedman, "Lesson of the Pencil," Liberty Pen, YouTube video, https://www.youtube.com/watch?v=4ERbC7JyCfU.

dumb buzzwords meant to confuse business owners. I don't ever accept deliverables. This means that I never fully sign off on projects. A great example is when I had Rick do the website. I never fully said yes and I never fully said no. It's important to keep projects and employees in limbo so that I remain in control.

This is not a mistake. It's good to keep all projects in a constant state of motion and not come to a grinding halt. It's never good to move on because it's important to understand that nothing is ever truly good enough. My employees must know that they can never satisfy me. If I say that something is good enough and complete a project, then I have taught my employees to be complacent in their work and I've taught them not to strive for the next best thing. I need to incentivize my employees to do better, and sometimes the best way to do that is by beating them down and telling them they're not good enough and that they never will be.

Now, I have to talk about paperwork since that's what most of project management is about.

FILES

I despise PDFs because I can't manhandle them. Someone once told me to try Adobe, but I don't eat Mexican. Fucking with files is the best way to embrace Spirit Tip #5: Keep Employees on Their Toes. Sabrina sent me a PDF of a document she created before her vacation, and I fired back at her a few days later demanding an editable version of the document. She made the document in Adobe (Mexican) InDesign, and I don't use InDesign, but that doesn't matter. I was furious that she sent me a PDF of her work. I called her the day she got cell phone reception in Grand Turk. I said "Sabrina, send me a word doc of the InDesign file." I could tell she didn't want to do it. But she did. I was actually surprised she sent me an email from the pool. Good for her.

I also hate PDFs because they don't always download properly. I can't download a PDF from Google Drive when Meghan shares it with me. I have repeatedly told her to email me a PDF and not to share it with me via Google Drive. She told me that was the same thing. What is she talking about? Sometimes I think these kids are so inundated with technology that they don't know a palm pilot from a BlackBerry.

FILE SHARING

Meghan prefers to use Google Drive. I tell her that I can't stand logging into my work Gmail just to view a file. Send it to my AOL email.

The glorious thing about Google Drive is that it's incredibly easy to fuck with files. Remember when I said that it's necessary to throw wrenches? Google Drive is my pride and joy for throwing wrenches. For example, I asked my 3D modelers to design a 2D pitch deck.

> Side Note: Artists despise making art outside their expertise. I don't know why this is a big deal. To me, art is art. My 3D artists whine all the time about doing graphic design and say they're not good at it. I don't know what that means other than they don't want to work.

They created it in Google Slides. Meghan shared the Google

Slides document with me and gave me editing access. A few days later, I said I couldn't find it (I purposefully deleted it). So, I called Meghan. She said she would look for it. Later, she called me and said that she couldn't find it. My modelers had to make an entirely new one. I threw a fit. I called Rick and told him that we needed to make sure that we store files where we know how to find them. After my modelers finished the new pitch deck (along with a few back-and-forth tweaks from me), Meghan sent me the file again, and I deleted it. I called her:

Me: "Meghan, it's gone again."

Meghan: "I'm not sure what happened."

Me: "We can't keep having this happen. Have them make it again. And quickly, I need to send it tomorrow."

Meghan emailed me later and said that Rick had downloaded it onto his machine. Later that day, I overheard my employees talking shit at the lunch table.

Rick: "I think he's purposefully deleting the files."

Meghan: "You think so?"

Sabrina: "That doesn't make any sense."

Dan: "Yeah, maybe he doesn't know how to use Google Drive."

Meghan: "He doesn't know how to open a PDF."

Rick: "I still think he's monkeying around."

Sabrina: "This has got to stop. It's too stressful."

Meghan sent me the Google Slides the next day. And again, I deleted it a few days later. I sent an email and CC'ed all of my employees:

Meghan,

If this happens again, I'll have to take action.

Meghan replied to me almost instantly with the Google Slides. Later, I learned via spy camera that they make copies of all files that they send to me. This proves that the tougher I am on my employees, the better they become. It's just like football. The tougher and more abusive the coach, the better the team. It's just that simple.

Concluding this chapter, project management is a necessary evil. It's a big waste of time but necessary for boondoggleness. I've detailed some genius ways of navigating the project management system in any business whether on the top or bottom. If you're on the bottom and you use these tips, then I'm certain that you'll be on the top soon.

THE BEST STRATEGY FOR GROWING A BUSINESS IS TO BUY TECH TOYS

CHAPTER 9

TECH & BIG DATA

I have no tolerance for nonsense, get away from me.
—*Tech N9ne*

THIS CHAPTER IS ABOUT two bogus concepts: technology and big data. They're bogus because there's so much hype around these two things. Whenever there's hype, there's bullshit involved. You can smell the bullshit from the large and fast cash burn from miles away. But, cash burn in tech and big data isn't always a bad thing if done for the right reasons.

The best strategy for growing a business is to buy tech toys. The more tech I can have in my business, the better my strategy and competitive advantage is. It doesn't matter if my employees can actually use the technology; what matters is that my facility has it. I can always find someone that can use software. Finding people to hire is the least of my problems.

> Side Note: Some fancy pants HR person would have you call people "human capital" because people are an asset to your business. This is dehumanizing. My employees are not assets, and there's certainly no value to them.

My people do what I need them to do and that's it. If they can't cut the mustard, then the mustard cuts them.

Accumulating tech toys is like rummaging through a grocery store: I'm looking for technology to feed to my employees. Employees are just like kids, and no one ever asks kids what they want from the grocery store because all they will tell you is dessert. Similarly, I never buy software that I know my employees have used before, because that gives them an advantage over me. If everyone can't use the software, including me, then I have the authority because I bought the software. It's important that my employees don't think I'm manipulating them. So, I always buy two different softwares that do the same thing so that my employees can test them and duke it out over which they prefer. It's my way of allowing them to think they have a choice. For instance, I purchased Adobe Creative Suite AND all the other tech to match: to compete with Adobe Premiere, I purchased an AVID system. To duke it out with Adobe Audition, I purchased ProTools (even though my studio doesn't really do sound.) To challenge employees that prefer Adobe Photoshop and Adobe Animate, I bought Harmony's ToonBoom (even though we mostly do 3D animation). Finally, and my favorite, to pit my employees against each other, I asked Rick to install both Autodesk Maya and Blendr. Rick tells me that using different softwares makes rendering the final product impossible, but I tell him that's his job to figure out. He doesn't know that I want as much software as possible to create division among the staff. The goal is to have the employees almost bring the company down so that I can step in and play savior. Besides, it gives me credibility when I threaten Sabrina that I'm going to shut the place down. It's fun to watch her squirm.

Another reason that I buy all these softwares is to keep my technology acceptance rate among my employees at an all-time low. I mean *Guinness-Book-of-World-Records* low. In business, the technology acceptance model (TAM), is a measure or process for how businesses roll out new tech and how willing their employees are to adopt the new tech. Usually, businesses want new tech roll outs to go smoothly. But I don't. I want my employees to hate the tech I buy because my business is a boondoggle and because I want my employees to be miserable. If my employees are miserable, then I can throw a furry party and have everyone love me.

Sometimes I buy hardware. Like when I dropped $200,000 on a server. The studio already had one, but that's when Rick was new, and I wanted him to have something to do. I wanted him to prove himself to me. I needed to make Rick figure out how to get all my shit off of the old server and transfer it to the new server. In testing Rick, I discovered that there was no accountability for the shit on the old server. I kept asking Rick where so-and-so was. His only reply was "there wasn't a system back then." What did he mean by that? Of course there was—it's called the old server. How could he not know where my shit was? I thought about suing him for incompetence and stealing my shit. Simply saying that he wasn't in charge when the old server was in use was not an excuse.

On another note, today's business climate is all about the "bleeding edge." It's a phrase invented by computer nerds so in love with horror films and games that they've incorporated this steamy passion into the business world that now relies heavily on technology. Disgusting, I know; but it just means that businesses are constantly adopting new technologies to stay on top of their game. I liken it to a football kicker that is constantly training his muscles and his brain to combat the pressures faced when kicking field goals. It takes a certain toughness to shut out the crowds and kick that pigskin.

Computer nerds have also inserted sex into business jargon. It's the people that get it the least that talk about it the most. Everything in business regarding big data* is about getting some. Specifically, it's about ass. That's why they call it "big" data.

Below is a list of nerd-talk-dirty-to-me jargon that's made its way into business:

1. Overfitting
2. Bias ("buy ass")
3. Bagging
4. Occam's Razor
5. Churn modeling
6. Persuasion modeling

I don't use big data in my business, because I think it's a waste of money. Gut instinct has always worked well for me. Because the purpose of this book is to stop answering everyone's goddamn questions, I will explain the realm of big data here. Before getting into the weeds with the dirty talk, I have to first explain how statistics and big data work together. Again, there is no math in this book because I hate math. Statistics isn't math at all but is really sorcery masquerading as math.

---

* "Big data is a term for data sets [groups] so large and complex that it becomes difficult to use traditional methods to capture, store, visualize, and analyze them." Norean Radke Sharpe, Paul F. Velleman, and Richard D. De Veaux, *Business Statistics*, 3rd ed. (Pearson, 2015), 830.

It is sorcery, because the nerds feed big data into a machine using a coding program and out pops a picture that lets them predict the future.

> Side Note: Pretty pictures that come from these nerds feeding their machines can define trends. This is where we get the color of the year and the next jean cut.

Below is an example of a picture that a nerd (AKA statistician, data scientist, virgin, etc.) likes to study for hours.

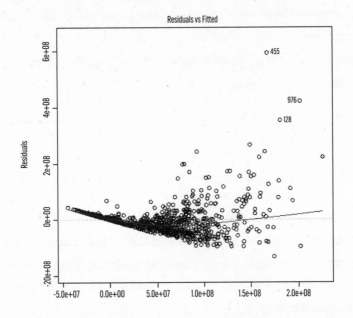

Doesn't look like much, but it's their porn. This is how it works: nerds feed their machines (coding) information (data) that they think would determine what they're trying to understand. The more information, the clearer the picture. The clearer the picture, the easier it is to spot trends and predict the future. Like I said: sorcery. But it's not as male-dominated of a field as you might expect: there is a lot of modeling involved.

> Side Note: Yes, men model, too, but not nearly as well as women. If you're a male statistician, make way for the women.

In statistics, the act of feeding a machine information and creating a picture is called modeling.

OVERFITTING*

The nerds will tell you to never overfit a model. I call bullshit. Overfitting is never a bad thing, because overfitting a model shows off all her assets. In my experience, tighter is always better.

BIAS†

Think "buy" ass. You can introduce bias by scurrying to your local brothel. I recommend ones you find in overnight diners. It's okay to buy ass. But don't buy ass with bias. I agree with the nerds on this one. Bias is a bad thing. Bias is preferring one ass to the next. It's weighing your options in the form of your own prejudices. **All ass is good ass except bias,** and don't you forget it.

---

* Overfitting (overlearning) is a statistical pitfall in which too much information and/or extraneous information is input into a data set to create a statistical model. It creates a model that indicates a relationship when one is not really there. E. Siegel, *Predictive Analytics* (Hoboken: Wiley, 2013), 120.

† Bias is introduced into a data set when only certain types of data are input into a statistical model based upon individual beliefs or preferences. Bias isn't always a conscious effort. Norean Radke Sharpe, Paul F. Velleman, and Richard D. De Veaux, *Business Statistics*, 3rd ed. (Pearson, 2015), 245.

BAGGING*

Bagging is when a nerd boinks three different sets of fraternal twins.

OCCAM'S RAZOR†

Nerds use Occam's Razor for foreplay. Something about sealing nerd love with a KISS.‡

CHURN MODELING§

Churn modeling is when a model goes to a homestead to churn butter for four hours instead of buying her butter from the store. It's stupid and hot.

---

* Bagging is short for bootstrap aggregating, which means that a diverse group of models based on different small groups of the same data set come together and decide what the best model is together. E. Siegel, *Predictive Analytics* (Hoboken: Wiley, 2013), 145.

† The simple answer is usually the right answer. An argument in statistics against overfitting (overlearning). *Encyclopaedia Britannica Online,* Academic ed., s.v. "Occam's Razor," by Brian Duignan, accessed October 7, 2020, https://www.britannica.com/topic/Occams-razor.

‡ "Keep it simple, stupid!" The juxtaposition between Occam's Razor and the KISS acronym is not the author's original idea. E. Siegel, *Predictive Analytics* (Hoboken: Wiley, 2013), 128.

§ Churn modeling predicts which customers are going to stop buying from Company A and switch to Company B. E. Siegel, *Predictive Analytics* (Hoboken: Wiley, 2013), 188.

PERSUASION MODELING*

Persuasion modeling is when a model tricks you into buying something that you didn't know you were going to buy. A model once sent me a coupon for a wax center. I saw the coupon, blinked, and the next thing I know I'm getting my balls stripped. I told that story to a guy in Charlottesville, Virginia, once. He said that the coupon influenced me, persuaded me to do the thing I was already thinking about doing. But I am not influenceable or persuadable because being influenced is sorcery, and I am not a wizard. (I was called a whiz kid in middle school, but that was because I peed on all my bullies.)

HONORABLE MENTIONS TO THE SEXY JARGON INCLUDE:

Meta-learning, which is learning on top of learning. Double the learning, double the fun.[†] It's also called ensemble. It is used to randomly copy some of the information that the nerds put into the machine. It's supposed to imitate real life. Nothing ever imitates real life.[‡]

Internet of Things (IoT) AKA "instrumentation of

---

* Persuasion modeling, also known as uplift modeling, predicts persuasion or whether a person, place, or thing is influenceable.

Eric Siegel, "The Persuasion Paradox- How Computers Optimize Their Influence on You," Elder Research (blog), July 5, 2019, https://www.elderresearch. com/blog/persuasion-paradox.

E. Siegel, *Predictive Analytics* (Hoboken: Wiley, 2013), 215-217.

† This is a reference to the Wrigley's Doublemint Gum marketing campaigns from the 1980s.

‡ E. Siegel, *Predictive Analytics* (Hoboken, NJ: Wiley, 2013), 140-144, 174.

anything." * This means that nerds like to stick it everywhere and in everything they can—all to get that big data. The debate about an "Internet of Things" world is what women know a lot about: consent and privacy. Nerds tap everything they legally can in your life to know everything about you and to predict which things to sell to you. IoT is like legalizing Big Brother (from the book, not the tv show, kids). This brings me to predictive analytics, which is using big data to predict what you will do. This is a good thing (definitely not a privacy issue), because it makes your miserable life slightly more comfortable. Instead of looking for a romantic partner, one that you will probably like is recommended for you.

> Side Note: The nerds use data for all sorts of things besides predicting what you will do. All my MBA students come crying to me when their finance professor teaches them R (the most popular statistical software in use now) and tells them to build a Black-Scholes option pricing model. In statistics, there's even an approach called Monte Carlo that incorporates some sort of random sampling into the modeling process. All this is fancy nerd lingo is usually named after a nerd or a bunch of nerds and the most recent trip they went on.

My goal for this chapter is to stop answering questions about tech and big data. But I also want to show that anyone can do what the nerds do as long as you're a nerd. I don't personally find it useful in my business, but plenty of others do. With a little grit, you can be just as successful as me.

---

* E. Siegel, *Predictive Analytics* (Hoboken: Wiley, 2013), 75.

ALL ASS
IS GOOD ASS
EXCEPT BIAS

CHAPTER 10

LEADERSHIP

My presence is a present—kiss my ass.
—Kanye West

LEADERSHIP IS A many-splendored thing. Just kidding—it's a scam. There are so many books written, seminars given, and classes taken dedicated to this ethereal thing called "leadership." My readers might even have purchased this book with the hope that I would give leadership advice. Here's the thing, there are two types of people in this world: leaders and followers. All babies are born into either category. It is not possible for a follower to become a leader.

Those in academia in leadership or management would have you believe that there are several different types of leadership. They suggest that leaders should understand what type of leadership they most align with and tailor their leadership styles to each person and situation.

LEADERSHIP STYLES

1. Trait Approach
2. Skills Approach

3. Behavioral Approach
4. Situational Approach
5. Path-Goal Theory
6. Leader-Member Exchange Theory
7. Transformational Leadership
8. Authentic Leadership
9. Servant Leadership
10. Adaptive Leadership*

Ten views on anything is overthinking, and overthinking is bad for business. It's bullshit to study leadership because it's so simple. Tell people what to do. That's it. If a person doesn't feel comfortable telling people what to do, then that person is not a leader.

Then there's servant leadership, which is what I call the "Christ Complex." Subscribers to servant leadership want to be like Jesus and do some feet washing. This is where the phrase "lead by example" comes from. I'll give an example, if even Jesus Christ can't paint a clear enough picture of what servant leadership is. Don runs a brothel. Don is a servant leader. He believes that in order to truly understand how to build a business with the highest value proposition for his clients and a healthy work environment for his girls, he has to pimp himself out too. Now let me ask you: does this make Don a leader, or does this make Don a gigolo?

Some may argue that servant leadership could be adapted by a born follower, which would make the follower a servant leader or (worse) a leader. This is just more "academic" mumbo jumbo that causes students to waste their time and

---

* P. G. Northouse, *Leadership: Theory and Practice*, 8th ed. (Los Angeles: SAGE, 2019).

money on thinking thoughts instead of doing real things.

> Side Note: I despise academia. That's why I teach at
> and am on the board of trustees at a prestigious uni-
> versity. I'll give you a little hint on which university I'm
> a trustee for: it may or may not include the word *the*
> in the title. I'm trying to bring the academic bastards
> down. We should dissolve all the colleges and universi-
> ties and make all the kiddos go to trade schools.

The word *leadership* indicates that there is one leader, and he is driving the ship. I get all sorts of questions about leadership because I'm a natural-born leader. But I can't tell people how to lead, because I don't know how everyone was born and what everyone is trying to do. (Usually babies that are born late are leaders.) The only thing I can say is if you're born a leader, go with your gut and never look back.

Authentic leadership is popular right now. Politicians and celebrities compete to be more authentic. There is nothing more inauthentic than talking about how authentic you are. But on the authenticity scale, I'm authentic as fuck. Stamping a person as authentic means that they are who they say they are. Authentic people "work on themselves" to be the best people that they can be, and authentic leaders help others with their own journey towards authenticity. This notion of authenticity is where we get weird sayings like "I need to find myself." To those people, I say, "Well, where the hell did you go?" You can't be conscious and not know where you are unless you're lost. If you're lost, then buy a compass.

Academics and business owners often confuse leadership and management. I repeat: leadership is telling people what to do. Management is hierarchy. Hierarchy is the number and type of positions in my company that have more responsibility. Academics teach that managers are leaders. In reality, managers are my pawns. I am the captain, and they are the crew. The difference between managers and employees under managers is that managers are more stressed out. Rick and Sabrina are my managers, and they think they're in a leadership role. I had to set them straight. They asked me if they could go to a leadership training at "the" university where I teach, and they wanted to use work time for it! I told them that they could go. Then on the day of the event, I requested several items from them to be sent to me by the end of the day. I saw via spy camera that they ended up not going. Good. I later asked them how the event went. They said it was a busy day, and I scolded them regarding time management. Leadership: it's telling people what to do for their own best interests and for the best interest of my company.

A note on mindfulness. Some management professors try to rope in graduate business students into practicing "mindfulness." If you scramble the letters in mindfulness, you get "fun dems sin l," which stands for "Fun Democrats Sin a Little." Mindfulness preaches the restorative powers of meditation. I talked to one of the mindfulness professors where I teach, and he said that you can even meditate while driving. Going zen while driving is a recipe for a calm car crash. **Mindfulness is madness, and meditating is a mind trap.** It's about standing desks and yoga breaks for employees. If businesses actually instituted the kind of new wave office environment that's hip and cool, nothing would ever get done. I went to a new wave venture capitalist office down the street that had kegs stacked from floor to ceiling. Those guys don't do work, and they certainly don't implement the Five Factors of Boondoggleness (plus one).

TEN VIEWS
ON ANYTHING IS
OVERTHINKING

I hate the study of leadership, but I do like being a leader. I get free stuff and free food. I'm the belle of the ball. As a matter of fact, I'm all ball and the ball. I get asked for advice often, which is why I wrote this book. My favorite question that I'm asked is: "What would you tell your younger self?" My answer is always the same: "You're a baller, son." People also ask me if I have any regrets in life. That question astonishes me. Of course I have no regrets, because I don't do anything wrong. Truly, nothing is ever my fault, and I'm always left to mop up the mess that my employees have made. It's exhausting to be this perfect. Who are some of my favorite leaders? All of the greatest quarterbacks of all time. They throw the ball where it needs to go. That's the kind of leadership that I've always wanted. People being where I need them to be without saying a word.

I cannot talk about leadership without talking about the hot-Brit-posing-as-an-American dude spreading lies with his books, TED Talks, and diagrams, Simon Sinek. A self-proclaimed optimist, Sinek teaches that "people don't buy what you do they buy why you do it." He says *why* is the basis for everything. His diagram regarding the notion of *why* is what he calls the Golden Circle (to mimic the Golden Ratio and probably also the Golden Rule). His Golden Circle is a series of rings in which the word *why* is in the center, the word *how* is in the second circle, and the word *what* is in the outer circle. Everything starts with why. But not all that glisters is gold.*

Why is not the reason for a business. *Why* is a means to an end. The joker that said life's about the journey probably owns a sports car and has a fat bank account like me. Life and leadership are about achieving objectives. The reason you play a game is to win. And it doesn't matter how you play the game: what matters is what the score is and how much time is left. Your *why* is to win. I'm surprised that the notion of starting everything in life with the question "Why?" hasn't induced mass panic. I dare you to ask five people why they did something, and they will retreat in confusion and think you're a weirdo. Why did you buy that coffee? Why do you go home after work? Why won't you date me? Why do you look pregnant? Asking *why* is a surefire way to make like a toddler

* Simon Sinek, *Start With Why: How Great Leaders Inspire Everyone to Take Action* (New York: Penguin Group, 2009).

and get slapped in the face. Of course, if that's what you're into, then go ahead. And what about asking yourself why? You would create a fog of self-doubt. I never wonder why I do something because I know why I do the things I do: sex, money, and free food. Everyone could use more sex. I never know why I need more money; I just know that I do. And it's not that hard; more money means more fun. More fun usually means free food.

Instead of going by Sinek's Golden Circle of self-doubt, I've included what I call the Hoops of Happiness that will help you with your business:

Instead of starting with why, start with free food. A man's measure of success is determined by how much free food he gets. If people give you free food or host events that give you free food, then that means you're as close to being worshipped as you could be for any given human. There's a saying that says "Free food is next to godliness, and gods never need a bib for ribs." Always achieve the type of success that will give you free food. The money, fame, and power that go with being rich and owning a business are icing on the cake. The best part of status is how much free food there is. This is what Maslow's Hierarchy of Needs got wrong: people are always looking for food. The richer the food, the more status you have. Typically the higher status you have, the food gets richer and freer. Now I get invited to simply show up to places that have food. **When your food is no strings attached, then you know you've made it big.** People love having me around, and the best way to grab my attention is with a good plate of food. After you identify the path of least resistance for setting yourself up for a future filled with free food, it's necessary to hold your position. This is best achieved by questionable tax practices and low employee wages. Make no mistake: questionable tax practices trump low employee wages every time. Paying low employee wages are important to keeping a fat stack of cash in the bank, but sometimes you have to pay people a little more to achieve boondoggleness. It's also fun to hire the best people to deal with my shit. Literally. Questionable tax practices will keep money in your pocket. Get yourself a good accountant, but one that does not question you. If it's legal, then it's doable. I use the tax laws to my advantage, and you should too.

MINDFULNESS IS MADNESS, & MEDITATING IS A MIND TRAP

WHEN YOUR FOOD IS NO STRINGS ATTACHED, THEN YOU KNOW YOU'VE MADE IT BIG

CHAPTER 11

STARTING A START-UP

Believe it or not, I swear I'm just a human being.
—Nelly

THERE ARE BEAUCOUP BOOKS on entrepreneurship, business models, value proposition, and being lean* as opposed to fat. Hell, this book is one of them. What those books typically provide is some sort of method and exercises for executing a fail-safe set of steps for starting a business. Those guys just want to sell books like me, but I'll tell you the real way to start a start-up.

At *the* university where I teach, the "Business Model Canvas" is one of the teaching pillars for all students on the entrepreneurship track. The canvas, or as I call it the "Incongruent Collage of Bullshit," is a giant sheet of paper divided into the following disproportionate boxes:

---

* *Lean* is a term applied to a way to operate a business start-up or department with as little waste as possible, *waste* being a subjective term.

1. Customer Segments
2. Value Propositions
3. Channels
4. Customer Relationships
5. Revenue Streams
6. Key Resources
7. Key Activities
8. Key Partnerships
9. Cost Structure*

These books encourage users to minimize words, even to draw pictures. I see students, managers, and consultants fall into the SWOT trap I mentioned back in Chapter Seven. They fill out these intriguing pieces of paper without understanding why they are doing it or what the fancy lingo means. And that means they are doomed to fail. Sexy paperwork and sleek designs are not the tools needed to start a start-up.

These minimalist business books will tell you to start with a business model to answer such questions as "What problem am I trying to solve?"; "Who will buy this product and why?"; and "How will I market and distribute my product to my target market?" First, the phrase "business model" is appalling. No business has that good of a reputation or operation going that should serve as a "model" for me or anyone else. I don't care if you're God Almighty trying to sell me a Bible: no business is worth the effort in being picked apart by pimple-popping pricks that dream of working in Wall Street. That's also why I hate model homes. I don't tolerate builders telling me what my house should look like, and I certainly won't stand for

---

*Alexander Osterwalder and Yves Pigneur, *Business Model Generation* (Hoboken: John Wiley & Sons, 2010).

anyone telling me how to operate my business.

There are way too many questions to answer in these books to complete the "business model." Business is not journalism. You don't need to know the who, what, where, when, and why. One of these sleek books that want you to ask a ton of questions is called *The Lean Startup*. The author, Eric Ries, talks about the Five Whys. The Five Whys aren't even his idea; he just talks about how brilliant he thinks it is.

> Side Note: The Five Whys comes from Toyota and is also called root-cause analysis. The last time I heard someone tell me I needed root-cause analysis, I was getting my tooth pulled in the back of a Tacoma in Costa Rica.

He says that to get to the bottom of a problem, management should ask "Why?" five times in order to determine where the true problem lies. In his opinion, problems are usually rooted in processes and not in people. If you think I disagree with that, you're right. Not because I hate people, but because I hate questions more. That's the reason I wrote this book, remember? I wrote this book so that I could stop answering everybody's goddamn questions. I hate when people question me. And that's what Eric wants—for young people to read his book and pester the crap out of their managers. I promise: you don't need to ask or answer questions to start a start-up.*

---

*Eric Ries, *The Lean Startup*, 1st ed. (New York: Crown Business, 2011).

I've proved that "business model" is a stupid term. Instead, I say abizmul. Abizmul stands for

A

biz (short for business)

must

use

luck

There's only one thing an abizmul needs: money. The trick is finding the money. There are a few ways to find money for an abizmul:

1. Get born rich
2. Fuck rich
3. Marry rich
4. Trick rich

I would suggest "Kill rich," but that indicates you probably already married rich or got born rich or even fucked rich to make the killing make you permanently rich. Of the above, I did number four. If you don't have money, then you will have an abysmal abizmul. And that truly is abysmal.

To start an abizmul start-up, find money and go with your gut. In conclusion, start up a start up with money.

CHAPTER 12

CLOSING COMMENTS

Being dead broke is the root of all evil.
—Rick Ross

I HOPE THIS BOOK teaches you to be more like me. I've discussed real business issues that some CEOs are too pussy-ass to talk about. If you have any more questions, do not ask me. If you meet someone with business questions, tell them to buy this book. Do not give your copy to them. I repeat: do NOT give your copy to them. Keep this book with you always, and I promise this book will be a resource to you.

If your boss does anything contrary to what I say in this book, then buy him a copy and slap him in the face with it. As he recovers from the shock of the book slap, tell him I say "Hi." If your boss is a woman or queer, then still buy the book, but instead of slapping the face, slap the ass. And instead of "Hi" tell them that I say "Hey."

It is my hope that this book makes it on a banned book list or is bold enough to make it to a book burning. Harnessing hate is like harnessing a power source no scientist has discovered yet. The more you hate me, the more influence I have. I'm fine with a good book burning as long as there's free food and fuzzy costumes. Hell, that's a party.

I do encourage you to read the people that I've badgered in this book so you can see for yourself that I'm right about what they say. Read Michael Porter. Watch Simon Sinek's TED Talks. Read an article on the power of analyzing big data. Dig deep. Grab a bite to eat. Then buy another copy of this book and pat yourself on the back for being smarter than your average bear.

I'm a furry.

THE
END

ACKNOWLEDGEMENT

IT'S SOMETIMES DIFFICULT to put into words how pleased I am with myself. But I'll try here. I would like to thank me for all of the cool things I've been able to do by myself. No one has helped me ever. Everything that I have accomplished in my life has been entirely in a vacuum and irrespective of "privilege."

> Side Note: "Privilege" is the modern buzzword for sour grapes. These people are jealous of my success because they are unable to work as hard as me. Well, I don't really work that hard: I'm just smarter than a lot of people. Hell, I'm a goddamn genius. A lot of people become angry when someone points the finger *Invasion-of-the-Body-Snatchers* style at their privilege. I don't get angry. When someone points out what they say is my "privilege," all they're really saying is that I'm successful and they're not. So instead of getting angry, I say, "Why yes, you're right. Sucks for you." This shuts them up immediately. I shock them when I agree with them at how much

of a loser they are compared to me. And I instantly get their respect.

It's great that I can build a dope life for myself. It's even better that I can get paid to make my rich self even richer. If **the purpose of an American life is to accumulate wealth as quickly as possible by punching down,** then I've done that pretty well. All by myself. It's not been easy, but it was worth it. Life is pretty sweet. My only fear is that on my deathbed I'll wish I had worked more.

THE PURPOSE OF AN AMERICAN LIFE IS TO **ACCUMULATE WEALTH** AS QUICKLY AS POSSIBLE **BY PUNCHING DOWN**

GLOSSARY OF TERMS

ABIZMUL: **A biz** (short for business) **must use** luck.

ANALYSIS OF ANALYSIS: Making plans to make plans to make plans.

BAGGING: When a nerd boinks three different sets of fraternal twins.

B CORP: Bad corp. A group of hippies getting high and pissing money away on recycled contact lenses all in the name of the uh-oh word.

BIAS: It's always ok to buy ass. It's never ok to discriminate against which ass you buy. Just be happy you got some.

BOONDOGGLENESS: The secret sauce to business success. There are five factors of boondoggleness, plus one.

CHRIST COMPLEX: A more apt term for servant leadership.

CHURN MODELING: When a model goes to a homestead to churn butter for four hours instead of buying her butter from the store. It's stupid and hot.

HOOPS OF HAPPINESS: A business should pay low employee wages and adopt questionable tax practices in order for its owners and shareholders to gain access to as much free food as possible. How much free food a man gets is the best way to measure his success.

INCONGRUENT COLLAGE OF BULLSHIT: Otherwise known as the Business Model Canvas.

INTERNET OF THINGS (IOT): Legalizing Big Brother (from the book, not the show).

META-LEARNING: An orgy in which people are stacked like pancakes on top of each other. It's the best type of learning on top of learning.

MINDFULNESS: Fun dems sin 1 or "Fun Democrats Sin a Little."

OCCAM'S RAZOR: A game of strip tease that nerds use during foreplay.

ORGANIZATIONAL CHANGE MANAGEMENT (OCM): It's a bullshit term. I go by Gandhi: be the change I want in my own company.

OVERFITTING: Making a model wear clothing that fits her. Make her wear that tight shit.

PERSUASION MODELING: When a model dupes you into spending money on something for yourself that you don't want.

PREDICTIVE ANALYTICS: A slick way of nerds trading your privacy for convenience, but poor people don't need privacy.

SUSTAINABILITY: Uh-oh.

SWOT TRAP: Suckers-With-Only-Time. Pseudo marketing analysis that allows those that swear by SWOT Analysis to seem like geniuses.

TELEPHONE: As in, the game: the only way to communicate in a business. If everything is he said–she said, then there is no liability. He said–she said is necessary for promoting rape culture and patriarchal precedents.

UH-OH WORD: Sustainability.

WORK-FOR-HIRE: The ability to own everything your employees say, think, and do while they work.